You Are
Special
You Were Chosen

My husband, Father Gayle, baptized Joanna and we both
knew her parents well. They were two who treasured
their adoptive daughter. *You Are Special-You Were Chosen*
comes from their hearts, too. The book is a wonderful
legacy they and Joanna have given to the world.

Anne Gayle

Joanna Ferlan
and
Mary Fox Prather

Mary Fox Prather

Joanna Tew

This book belongs to:

_____

Published by Tate Publishing & Enterprises, LLC
127 E. Trade Center Terrace | Mustang, Oklahoma 73064 USA
1.888.361.9473 | www.tatepublishing.com

Tate Publishing is committed to excellence in the publishing industry. The company reflects the philosophy established by the founders, based on Psalms 68:11,
"The Lord gave the word and great was the company of those who published it."

Book design copyright © 2007 by Tate Publishing, LLC. All rights reserved.
Original illustration concepts by Ling Andreasson
Cover design & illustrations by Kathy Hoyt
Interior design by Lynly D. Taylor

Published in the United States of America

ISBN: 978–1-6024727–4-7
1. Children's Family   2. Adoption
07.08.22

To adoptive children everywhere

Foreword

Joanna and Mary are the co-authors of a new book, *You Are Special—You Were Chosen*; but the material comes from the heart of an adoptive father.

When Joanna was first adopted, her dad wrote a similar story to their book. He told Joanna this story every night before she went to sleep. She grew up feeling very special— almost sorry for those not adopted.

As Joanna and Mary have grown older, they met many adults who were adopted as children. These adults lack the self assurance Joanna has developed. She attributes her positive outlook to the message from this story.

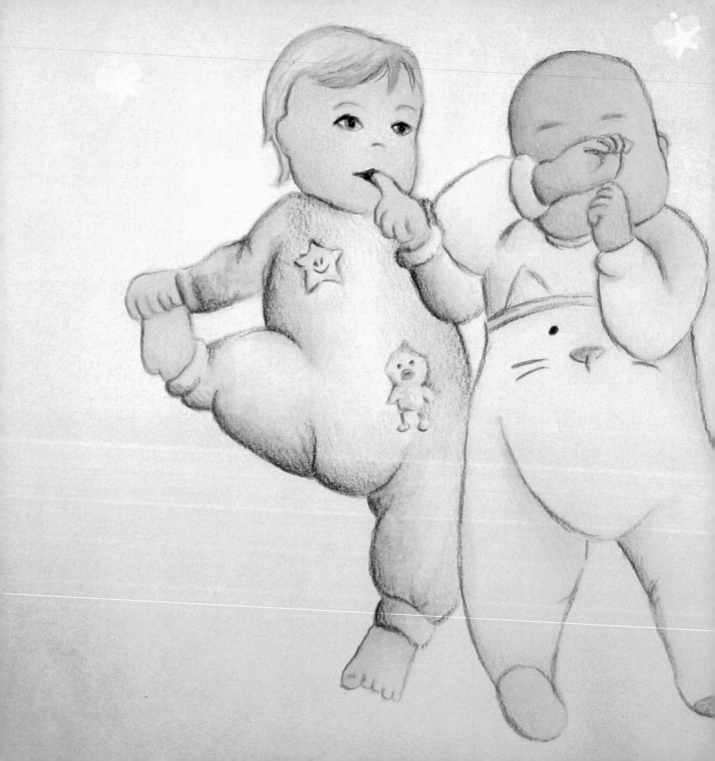

Each of us is special
with a guardian angel
among the stars.

Do you ever **wonder**...

what makes you "extra" special?

Once upon a star your guardian angel was **born**.

She **knew** your birth mom and new mom.

Long before your two moms knew you were going to be a **gift**, the angel had a **plan**.

Out of her **love** for you,

she **created** you in the angel's garden of stars.

Then she **sent** you to earth.

For **nine** months your birth mom did her job.

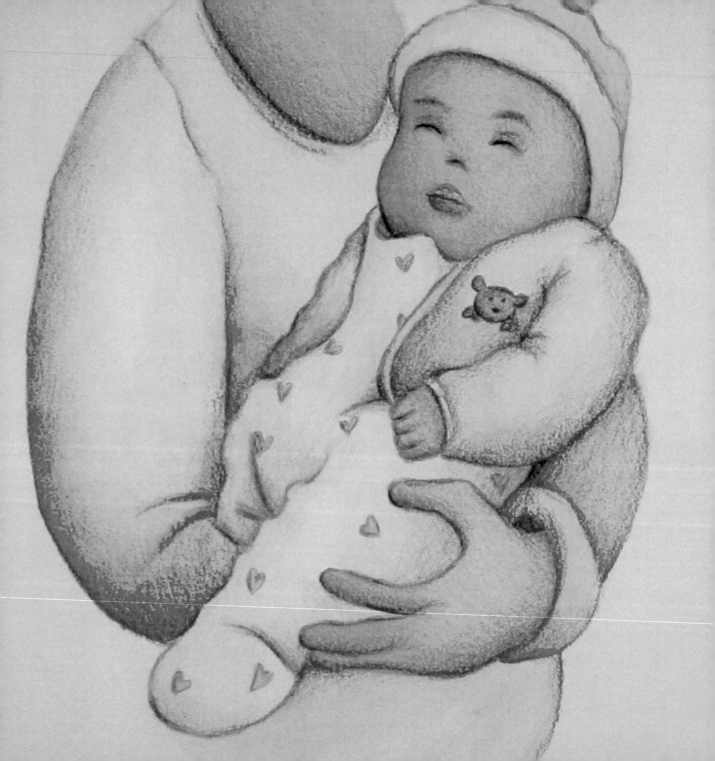

You grew inside her tummy
where you were protected and fed.

After you were **born**,

she had the **courage** to give you a better life.

Waiting was a family full of love to give to you.

Everyone in the family knew how **special** you were
and wanted the **best** for you.

So here you are! Wanted and loved by **many**.

But in **every** family there are times when you feel sad or alone.

So if you ever feel lonely, your angel has a **poem** for you.

At night if you are **feeling** sad or blue and

feel that your **family** isn't part of you

Look at the **stars** and know from the start

You were created and loved in **many** a heart.

I know that this is **true**,

because I was **chosen** just like you.

What Else Makes YOU Special?

singing   gymnastics   hugger   braces

_____

green
eyes   good
listener   brown
hair   socce
playe

_____

cute
smile   horseback
rider   blonde
hair   playing an
instrument

_____

football
player   caring   good
speaker   freckle

_____

polite   skateboarder   brown
eyes   curls

_____

good at
sports   black hair   a
reade

_____

good student	friendly	blue eyes	straight hair

laughing	responsible	good at math	dancer

funny	tall	baseball player	black eyes

short	understanding	good smile	chosen

skier	hard worker	love animals	is kind

volleyball player	know more than one language	flexible	

e|LIVE

listen|imagine|view|experience

AUDIO BOOK DOWNLOAD INCLUDED WITH THIS BOOK!

In your hands you hold a complete digital entertainment package. Besides purchasing the paper version of this book, this book includes a free download of the audio version of this book. Simply use the code listed below when visiting our website. Once downloaded to your computer, you can listen to the book through your computer's speakers, burn it to an audio CD or save the file to your portable music device (such as Apple's popular iPod) and listen on the go!

How to get your free audio book digital download:

1. Visit www.tatepublishing.com and click on the e|LIVE logo on the home page.
2. Enter the following coupon code:
   e99e-9216-620e-626b-f950-cdb0-df0e-a732
3. Download the audio book from your e|LIVE digital locker and begin enjoying your new digital entertainment package today!